The Brave Monk

ISBN# 1-930710-36-4
Copyright ©2000 Veritas Press

Veritas Press
1250 Belle Meade Drive
Lancaster, PA 17601

First edition

Written by R.C. Sproul, Jr.
Illustrated by Mark Ammerman

The Brave Monk

Veritas Press

To Michael, Anna, Bobby, Scott, Marbin,
Sarah, Jessa, Skipper, Kacey, Christopher,
Nick, Lizzie, Stephanie, Tiffany, Cydney,
adopted unto life.
—R.C. Sproul, Jr.

Martin Luther was a monk.

Monks spent time with the Bible
and singing to God.

While Martin was alive,
no one but monks and some men
were able to get to the Bible.

When Martin spent time with the Bible,
it said things that were not what the Church
said. The Bible said that all men must put

I am the Way, the Truth and the Life. Nobody comes to the Father but by me.

...t be good so that God will love ...u must keep all the laws of God ...is church.

their hope and trust in Jesus alone to have life with God. The men of the Church had said that men must work hard to be holy and for God to love them.

Did Martin dare to go tell men what the
Bible said? Martin was a brave monk.
On one paper he wrote a list of

95 bad things that the Church had said. He
hung the list in the square to share with
others what the Bible said.

As men came to work or trade wares, they were able to pore over Martin's list. They said the Church was silly, and Martin was wise. The other monks felt anger.

They bade Martin to debate with them.
Martin went to debate with the Churchmen.
Many angry monks sat fixing stares on him.

"Did you write this list, Brother Martin?"
they said, trying to scare him. The plan was
to get men to do what the Church said,
not what the Bible said.

"Yes," said the brave monk,
"I wrote that paper."

The angry monks said, "You must be silent
and state these things no more, and so spare
the public your mistakes.

You must take back the things you have said. You cannot be correct, when the Church tells us you are not.

You are to blame for those who will not submit to the Church, but abide by the Bible, and hope and trust Jesus alone to save them. Are you sorry?" they did inquire.

I am not ashamed of the Gospel of Christ, for it is the power of God unto Salvation.

Martin felt as if he were a hare stuck in a snare. He did implore God to help him, to help him be brave. Was he sorry?

Brave Martin said, "I do not care that you have such anger. I can not be silent. I must relate what the Bible has said.

Strike me with your blades; hit me with
your spades. I will not state that I am sorry.
Here I stand. I can act in no other manner.
So help me God."

Did the brave monk fare well? Did the other
monks smite him? He ran from the
assembly, into the late evening shade.

A man did grab him, and put Martin on his mare, before going off into the forest. Was he one of the angry monks?

No, it was a man close to Brother Martin,
and he sent him to a safe fortress.
From there the rare monk wrote on paper
many things, telling many men the plan

to have never-ending life with God. He did
want all men to be able to spend time with
the Bible and to note what God has said.

Martin Luther was a brave monk
for he did revere God.

Martin put his hope and trust
in Jesus alone to save him, and he had
never-ending life with God.

Those who love God
give thanks for the
brave monk Martin,

for he did state what the Bible said
and did not take it back.